Rooted & Wild

A DEVOTIONAL for ADVENTUROUS WOMEN

Joy Scarpuzzi

Published by Made to Change the World™ Publishing
Nashville, Tennessee

ISBN: 978-1-956837-53-7 (paperback)
ISBN: 978-1-956837-54-4 (ebook)

Printed in the USA, Canada, Australia, and Europe

Dedication

To God, who inspires me with His creation, love, and providence.

To my main adventure buddies, Aunt Kyrie, Becky, and Carol:
I literally could not have done it without you.

To my family, Joanna, Jon, Zoey, Mom, and Dad:
Thank you for encouraging the way God has gifted me.

To my Southern California and Alaska ECO family:
Without your support, I wouldn't have made it
through some of the darkest days of my life.

ADVENTURES in PSALMS

HOW TO USE
THIS DEVOTIONAL

Every day, you will be encouraged to read a psalm and perhaps another passage.

Each day includes a key verse with a theme. Feel free to memorize that verse or write it on a note to look at throughout the day.

A prayer is provided for you to pray each day, but there is also space for you to write your own prayer or any thoughts that come to you.

I love to write down my prayers, so I encourage you to do the same. Not every day will reflect or correlate with what you're going through, but ask the Holy Spirit to show you what He wants you to take away from His word each day.

I'm praying for you, sister!

Let's wander in nature with God!

He is like a tree planted by streams of water that yields its fruit in its season, and its leaf does not wither. In all that he does, he prospers.

—Psalm 1:3 (ESV)

Day 1

BE A TREE

Read Psalm 1.

Have you ever seen a tree thriving in the middle of nowhere? Surrounded by sandy ground, it's a little confusing. How is this tree thriving while everything else around it is dying?

You guessed it—a hidden river runs beneath that tree. Its roots grow down deep into the soil. That's how this one tree prospers while all around it are drying up.

As you read the first chapter of Psalms, I think we all want to be called *blessed women*. Verse 2 tells us what to do, and verse 3 shows us the result of being connected to God—who is like a river that gives us life when all around us things are dying.

If we take a look at the world around us, pain, grief, and suffering are everywhere. If you're like me, you might question how we thrive in such a difficult world. It's simple—and yet not so simple—at the same time.

So, as we set off on this journey together, let's take time to meditate on God's word and take in His beautiful creation. My prayer for you, my dear sister, is that this devotional not only helps you connect with

God through the nature we find around us, but also becomes a daily starting point as you take delight in God's word.

So do not follow the crowd. Instead, delight yourself in God's word—not just once a week, or once a day, but morning and night.

Prayer

Take a deep breath and let your heart settle
as you pray the following prayer.

Creator God, the One who created the beautiful world around me, I yearn to be like a tree planted by streams of water. I long to be connected to You, to rest in You. Remind me today of Your goodness and Your sustaining grace and love for me. In Jesus' name, Amen.

Write a prayer or any thoughts that come to mind:

He is like a tree planted by streams of water that yields its fruit in its season, and its leaf does not wither. In all that he does, he prospers.
Psalm 1:3 (ESV)

*Be gracious to me, O Lord, for I am languishing:
heal me, O Lord, for my bones are troubled.*

—Psalm 6:2 (ESV)

TROUBLED BONES

Read Psalm 6 and Matthew 7:7-11.

Chances are, you've asked God for something and haven't received it. Maybe it was healing for yourself or someone you cared about. God's word tells us to ask, seek, and knock. You've done all those things, and yet, God hasn't answered your prayers the way you wanted Him to.

Praying can be tricky. We're told to pray about everything. There are days when every prayer gets answered immediately. Other times, years of praying seems to yield nothing. I get it—prayer can be frustrating.

That is, if we think the goal of prayer is to get things.

But the Bible tells us the goal of prayer isn't to get things—that's just an added perk.

The true goal of prayer is to know God.

When your bones are troubled—after a long hike or an emotionally draining day—talking with God can be the result of your dependence on Him, not a sign that your bones don't feel tired.

Don't misunderstand me: God loves it when we pray. He loves hearing from His daughters. But if the goal isn't to get to know God more, we've missed the whole point. Prayer changes us, as we grow closer to the God of the universe who loves us.

National park parking lots bring out a lot of prayers from me. "Lord, provide a parking spot for us," has been prayed silently, quietly, and—on occasion—shouted.

Nothing is too small or too big for God to handle. I think we feel more comfortable praying medium prayers than we do praying big and small prayers. But it's the small prayers that give us the confidence to know that we can ask a loving God to heal us when we are languishing—when the only thing that can help us is God.

Today, I want us to practice asking God for small, medium, and big things. Be confident in a God who wants to give you good things.

Prayer

Take a deep breath and let your heart settle
as you pray the following prayer.

God, in Your word, You tell us to pray about everything. Hear my prayers for the things that worry me, but more than answering my prayers, I ask Lord, that You would draw me closer to Your heart. Make my first reaction prayer instead of my last resort. I pray all this in Jesus' name, Amen.

Write a prayer or any thoughts that come to mind:

Be gracious to me, O Lord, for I am languishing: heal me, O Lord, for my bones are troubled. Psalm 6:2 (ESV)

When I look at your heavens, the work of your fingers,
the moon and the stars, which you have set in place,
what is man that you are mindful of him,
and the son of man that you care for him?
—Psalm 8:3-4 (ESV)

Day 3

STARGAZING

Read Psalm 8.

I still remember the first time I saw the stars on a dark night while driving home from a state park. I was young, but not too young to know that if I wanted to continue experiencing such beauty, I knew exactly who to go to: God. Sitting in the back of our Grand Voyager, I said a quick prayer. "Dear God, when I grow up, I want to live where the stars are."

At the time, I lived in the suburbs of the bustling city of Chicago. So the Illinois farmland where I whispered that prayer was such a stark contrast to the world I lived in.

Often, we can be so busy in our lives that we don't even notice God's handiwork around us. I want to encourage you right now—if you're not already outdoors—to step outside and take in the vastness of nature.

Verse 3 first reminds us who the heavens belong to. Did you catch that? *Your heavens.* Then it reminds us who created it all: *the work of your fingers.*

Everything around us has been set in place by our Creator. But verse 4 turns that introspection on us. For a God who could create all this, how is it that He cares so deeply for us?

Little did I know, God would not only provide a home for me where I could one day see the stars—but a place where I could even see the Northern Lights dance across the sky.

God knew me so well, He gave me more than I ever asked for—because He wanted to lavish His beautiful creation on me.

I was reminded of my smallness while watching the Aurora Borealis dance over the mountains. And that moment led to connecting with the Creator of those beautiful lights.

As you think about God's creation, what places and spaces remind you of your smallness? Ask God to use those moments to help remind you of just how loved you are.

Prayer

Take a deep breath and let your heart settle
as you pray the following prayer.

Dear God, thank you for Your beautiful creation and how it always draws me into a relationship with You. I will never understand why You are mindful of me. And yet, my heart is filled with gratitude for Your goodness. Thank you for caring so deeply for me. Even now, You know my needs before I utter them. Allow my heart to fill with Your peace and comfort. In Jesus' name, Amen.

Write a prayer or any thoughts that come to mind:

When I look at your heavens, the work of your fingers, the moon and the stars, which you have set in place, what is man that you are mindful of him, and the son of man that you care for him?
Psalm 8:3-4 (ESV)

How long, O Lord? Will you forget me forever?
How long will you hide your face from me?
How long must I take counsel in my soul
and have sorrow in my heart all the day?
—Psalm 13:1-2 (ESV)

Day 4

HOW LONG?

Read Psalm 13.

The first question any good hiker asks before setting out on a hike is: *How long is this hike?*

The next one is: *Is the trail out and back or a loop?* We need to know the duration in order to make an educated decision about whether we want to go.

The psalmist is pleading with God: *How long will you seemingly hide from me? How long will this waiting season last?*

We've asked the same questions in life. Wouldn't it be so much easier if God said, *You will go through this difficult time for three months. In two months, you will want to give up—but hold on. I will answer your prayers in three months.*

I wish He would give us a timeline for the painful situations in our lives.

But reading this chapter should give us hope. The psalmist begins with this desperate plea, but he ends the chapter with a hopeful decree: *I have trusted your steadfast love.*

One of the many reasons why I love reading the psalms is because the writer is honest with God about what is going on in his life. The way he prays—cries out—to God is so real. He doesn't hide what he's feeling in the moment. He allows himself to experience a moment of utter despair.

In today's language, we would probably say he allowed himself to feel his emotions in that moment and shared what he was feeling with God.

Whether you are an internal processor or a verbal processor, prayer can be a great place to untangle your thoughts—with a God who unconditionally loves you.

Let the psalmist set the example for you. God can handle your feelings. Just remember: You can trust God to come through—because He has come through time and time again in your life.

Prayer

Take a deep breath and let your heart settle
as you pray the following prayer.

Dear God, I relate to the psalmist asking how long. Sometimes it feels like You're far away or that You're ignoring me. It's a painful feeling. Please bring to mind, in those moments, all the times You have come through in my life so that I know You'll never leave me and that You hear my prayers. God of comfort, be close to me today. In Jesus' name, Amen.

Write a prayer or any thoughts that come to mind:

How long, O Lord? Will you forget me forever? How long will you hide your face from me? How long must I take counsel in my soul and have sorrow in my heart all the day? Psalm 13:1-2 (ESV)

I love you, O Lord, my strength.
The Lord is my rock and my fortress and my deliverer,
my God, my rock, in whom I take refuge, my shield,
and the horn of my salvation, my stronghold.
—Psalm 18:1-2 (ESV)

THE LORD IS MY ROCK

Day 5

Read Psalm 18 and 2 Corinthians 12:9.

King David wrote this psalm after God delivered him from King Saul. David goes on and on about how God saves him, using a bunch of nature imagery. He calls God his rock, fortress, and deliverer.

I can't even begin to imagine what it must have felt like to be chased by a king who wants to kill you—to always be worried that something is about to happen, and not by your own doing but because God put a calling on your life.

David calls God *my strength*.

Have you ever wanted to give up? Me too.

We all have days that we just want to sleep away, days we wish we could wake up and realize everything was just a dream.

But we weren't made to go through life alone. The Apostle Paul writes about this in his second letter to the Corinthian church. In the 12th chapter, he begs God to take away his "thorn." We're not sure what Paul's thorn was, but it was something that hindered him.

He begged God to take it away. Yet God tells him, *My grace is sufficient for you, for my power is made perfect in weakness.* God told him—and tells us—that our weaknesses are not something we should be ashamed of. Instead, they should remind us that God's power is made perfect in our weakness, that our lack of strength is actually a gift because it means we have to rely on God.

Paul then writes the words that are so hard to believe: *Therefore I will boast all the more gladly about my weaknesses, so that Christ's power may rest on me.* Our culture tells us to hide our weaknesses, to hope no one sees them. But Paul says *boast in them,* because it means God is working through you.

What would it look like for us to boast in our weaknesses—for God to be our strength? What are the parts of us we wish we didn't have to deal with? How can we accept the parts of us that are weak, trusting that God's strength will be evident in our lives through them?

Prayer

Take a deep breath and let your heart settle
as you pray the following prayer.

Dear God, I cannot do it all. I need Your strength in my moments of weakness. Be the rock I can lean on when I don't have the energy to keep going. Remind me that I am Your daughter and You are my deliverer. In Jesus' name, Amen.

Write a prayer or any thoughts that come to mind:

I love you, O Lord, my strength. The Lord is my rock and my fortress and my deliverer, my God, my rock, in whom I take refuge, my shield, and the horn of my salvation, my stronghold.
Psalm 18:1-2 (ESV)

The Lord is my Shepherd; I shall not want.
He makes me lie down in green pastures.
He leads me beside still waters. He restores my soul.
He leads me in paths of righteousness for his name's sake.

—Psalm 23:1-3 (ESV)

Day 6

MY SHEPHERD

Read Psalm 23 and John 10:1-20.

Sister, take a long breath in, and then breathe slowly out. You've made it to one of the most famous psalms. Maybe you've read this psalm next to a sheep or in a green pasture as the sun warmed your face. I'm praying that if you're in a windowless room, you are feeling the warmth too.

The Lord is my Shepherd....

I have a suspicion about this chapter and why it's so popular. It's because it speaks to us in *whatever* season of life we are in.

In this big world, we can often feel alone—like we're the only one walking the path we're on. Yet this chapter reminds us that we are not alone. We aren't just walking aimlessly; we have a Shepherd who guides, protects, and gently leads us.

When Jesus teaches His disciples, He tells them He is not just any shepherd. *I am the Good Shepherd.* Jesus tells us that He knows us— not just our names, but our tendencies.

A shepherd knows His sheep well. He knows which ones are always wandering off. He knows which ones aren't fully aware of their surroundings, and which ones can get easily entangled.

Talking with a mentor of mine, I said to him, "God just knows me." He laughed and sarcastically said, "That's great theology!" But what I meant to say is that God *knows me and loves me*, which many people don't feel is true in life. God knows my desires, and He doesn't just give me what I ask for; He often dumps extra blessings on me just to remind me that He knows me.

Prayer

Take a deep breath and let your heart settle
as you pray the following prayer.

My Good Shepherd, thank you that I never walk alone. You are right beside me in every situation—in the moments I'm too afraid to move and the moments all I want to do is dance. Remind my heart when I feel alone that You will never leave me. Good Shepherd, would you be close to me today? In Jesus' name, Amen.

Write a prayer or any thoughts that come to mind:

The Lord is my Shepherd; I shall not want. He makes me lie down in green pastures. He leads me beside still waters. He restores my soul. He leads me in paths of righteousness for his name's sake.
Psalm 23:1-3 (ESV)

Make me to know your ways, O Lord;
teach me your paths.
Lead me in your truth and teach me,
for you are the God of my salvation;
for you I wait all the day long.

—Psalm 25:4-5 (ESV)

WHAT'S MY PATH?

Read Psalm 25.

Have you ever gone on a hike without a map? Not only would that be unwise, but depending on your terrain, it could be deadly. On the flip side, have you ever gone on a hike where you simply have to...follow?

Some people use the phrase *turn your brain off*. I don't know about you, but that sounds scary—especially if you don't trust the person leading you. Imagine following a first timer as they lead you further and further from cell service. That would be a huge mistake.

But I want to remind you who is leading you. Yesterday, we were able to sit with our Shepherd—the One who knows us completely. He knows how to lead us with kindness, love, and strength. That is who is leading us on *His* paths.

In verse 3, we are told that those who wait for God are not put to shame. Sometimes, it's in the waiting that we get into the most trouble. We want to go faster. We try to get ahead of the Shepherd, ahead of our Guide.

If you've been hiking for a while, you're probably similar to me:

I cannot stand slow hikers or walkers. (I'm fully aware that I'm a slow hiker sometimes—but come on, people, pick up the pace!)

The theologian N.T. Wright says this about slowing down: "It is only when we slow down our lives that we can catch up to God."

Where in our lives do we need to slow down and let God lead us? If we want Him to teach us His path, we have to allow ourselves to be led by God at His pace, not ours.

Slow down, sister, so you can catch up with God.

Prayer

Take a deep breath and let your heart settle
as you pray the following prayer.

Dear God, I ask You to lead me, yet oftentimes I attempt to get ahead of You because I'm not willing to wait for You. Slow my heart down to catch up to You. This journey is not worth it unless I am walking with You. Remind me of Your goodness and that You can be trusted. My Shepherd, guide me. In Jesus' name, Amen.

Write a prayer or any thoughts that come to mind:

Make me to know your ways, O Lord; teach me your paths.
Lead me in your truth and teach me, for you are the God of my
salvation: for you I wait all the day long. Psalm 25:4-5 (ESV)

By the word of the Lord the heavens were made,
and by the breath of his mouth all their host.
He gathers the waters of the sea as a heap;
he puts the deep in storehouses.
—Psalm 33:6-7 (ESV)

Day 8
LOVE WE CAN SEE

Read Psalm 33.

Love is a hard thing to put your finger on. I love Persian food. I dream about *albaloo polo* (tart cherry rice with chicken). But if I had to choose between my sister or *albaloo polo*, I'd choose *albaloo polo*. Just kidding! I'd choose my sister.

The writer of this psalm tells us that the world is full of evidence of the steadfast love of the Lord. Then he begins to give us references from nature to prove his point.

I have a suspicion that you and I are similar in a way. When you are in nature, you connect with God. That's what makes us adventurers. We wouldn't do it unless we loved it. A couch is way more comfortable than hiking in the heat of the desert.

For me, being in nature is one of my favorite ways to connect with God. I love being reminded of how much He loves me as I look at the towering rocks around me or the depth of the Grand Canyon.

I hope you're currently in your favorite national park or on a nature walk, but if you're not, take a moment to think about that place. What about it reminds you of God's love?

Growing up in the endless cornfields of the Midwest states, I remember the first time I saw the Smoky Mountains, traveling in our green family van and being able to see for miles from the top of the mountains.

When I moved to Alaska, I saw the endless beauty surrounding me. Each morning, I would wake up amazed at God's love for me. A God who took the time to create such wonders for me to enjoy is a God I want to know more deeply.

So, your homework today is to open your eyes, look around at nature, and observe the handiwork of God. Thank Him for the love He put into creating the world around you.

Prayer

Take a deep breath and let your heart settle
as you pray the following prayer.

God, I look at Your creation and am amazed at the works of Your hand. Open the eyes of my heart to see Your love for me in the world You created around me. In Jesus' name, Amen.

Write a prayer or any thoughts that come to mind:

By the word of the Lord the heavens were made, and by the breath of his mouth all their host. He gathers the waters of the sea as a heap; he puts the deep in storehouses. Psalm 33:6-7 (ESV)

The Lord is close to the brokenhearted and saves those who are crushed in spirit.
—Psalm 34:18 (ESV)

Day 9

BROKENHEARTED

Read Psalm 34.

Have you ever been heartbroken? Relationships are the usual suspects when we get our hearts broken. But it could be dreams that you thought would happen, like a dream of who you wanted to become.

At nine, I thought I had my life planned out. I was going to be an athletic trainer for the Chicago Bears, married to the starting quarterback. You know—the dreams of a star-struck pre-teen. So when my parents announced that our family would be moving, I was devastated.

While I was still naive enough to be hopeful, I look back to that moment and remember being brokenhearted. I still grieve the life I wished I could've had.

So maybe it was a broken heart due to a friendship falling apart or it was a dream of your future self that didn't come true. Take heart, because God is near you.

I'm not sure how you deal with a broken heart. I've learned that a good *Lord of the Rings* marathon with warm soup is just what my soul needs. But I also need a reminder that when I'm brokenhearted, I'm not too much for my friends or for God.

We sometimes feel ashamed that heartbreak affects us so deeply, which can lead to isolation. When our feelings are all messed up, we often struggle to feel the truth that God is near. We want to hide and hope no one sees us.

Reaching out to a friend can be hard during this time, but God is near you. No matter what you feel right now, the Creator of the universe is near you. He is holding you as you cry, as you grieve. I pray you feel His great love for you in the midst of your heartbreak.

Prayer

Take a deep breath and let your heart settle
as you pray the following prayer.

Dear God, no part of me is hidden from You. You see my crushed heart, and You draw near to me. Allow my soul to find safety in You. Let my heart be reminded of Your great love for me. In the moments where You feel distant, show me the ways You are already working on my healing. Lord God, be near to me in tangible ways. In Jesus' name, Amen.

Write a prayer or any thoughts that come to mind:

The Lord is close to the brokenhearted and saves those who are crushed in spirit. Psalm 34:18 (ESV)

Your steadfast love, O Lord, extends to the heavens.
Your faithfulness to the clouds.
Your righteousness is like the mountains of God;
your judgments are like the great deep;
man and beast you save, O Lord.
—Psalm 36:5-6 (ESV)

Day 10
STEADFAST LOVE

Read Psalm 36.

The unwavering love of God extends to the heavens. As humans, our love can be conditional. The closest we may come to unconditional might be our love for family, a spouse or partner, or our kids. Yet we all reach a point where we wonder if it's possible to continue loving the other person.

One of my favorite things about God is that I can't do anything to make Him not love me. For me, it's the only relationship right now in which I feel both fully known and fully loved.

Love can be hard to comprehend—which is why I love that the psalmist uses the image of it reaching to the heavens. The righteousness of God is like the mountains, a visual representation of what it looks like—its power and permanence. Later in the chapter, we're told that God's steadfast love is precious and is a refuge.

If you're not currently near mountains, take a moment to visualize what it might look like for those mountains to represent God's steadfast love for you.

While living in Juneau, Alaska, there was one road out of town to

Berners' Bay. A little after that, you'd be greeted by an "End of the Road" sign. The mountains *restricted* travel in and out of Juneau—you could only come by boat or plane. Even across the bay, more mountain ranges loomed in the distance. There was no escaping the mountains.

Some days, I felt constricted by those mountains surrounding me. I felt claustrophobic, driving the narrow roads. But when I reflected on passages that describe mountains as places of safety, the way I looked at them began to change. They became a reminder of God's steadfastness and faithfulness in my life.

Prayer

Take a deep breath and let your heart settle
as you pray the following prayer.

Dear God, in a world that is changing everyday, we hear of wars and rumors of wars, people in need, and we experience pain. As we look to the mountains, would You remind us of Your great love for us? That unlike our world, You are unchanging and we claim Your promise to be a refuge. Hide me under Your wings today. In Jesus' name, Amen.

Write a prayer or any thoughts that come to mind:

Your steadfast love, O Lord, extends to the heavens.
Your faithfulness to the clouds. Your righteousness is like
the mountains of God; your judgments are like the great deep;
man and beast you save, O Lord. Psalm 36:5-6 (ESV)

Be still before the Lord and wait patiently for him.
—Psalm 37:7 (ESV)

Day 11

BE STILL

Read Psalm 37.

Do you ever avoid silence? Maybe you actually love sitting still and listening for God. I could blame it on my personality or how I'm wired, but sitting still just doesn't cut it for me. I think that's why I love being in nature so much—I often don't need noise when I walk in creation.

There's something about looking at the world around me that draws me closer to the God who created it all. I ask questions as I look at the flowers. While out in nature, stillness comes so easily to me. I see a verse that tells me to be still and patient, and while sitting on a rock overlooking a canyon, I can do that with ease.

But the moment I return to my apartment, it's noise and more noise. There is no stillness—unless I am reminded of the loneliness that often lingers in a home inhabited by just one person: me.

It's easy to connect with God in nature, but in my apartment, it's as if the walls that keep me safe from the outside world also block my connection to Him.

Maybe you're nothing like me, but odds are you might feel the same way. There are places in your life where it's hard to be still.

Wherever you find yourself today, I want to encourage you to be still. Stop striving. Just sit and watch what God is doing around you. Be still. Let Him fight the battle you're anxious about today.

Maybe stillness is foreign to you. Don't worry—God isn't asking you to sit and stare at a wall for an hour or it doesn't count. Start with five or ten minutes. You could even lie down, close your eyes, and just be still. Allow whatever thoughts come your way to pass, and gently set them aside by repeating the phrase, *Speak, Lord, for your servant hears.* (1 Samuel 3:10)

Prayer

Take a deep breath and let your heart settle
as you pray the following prayer.

Lord, as I sit in stillness, be near. Hear the prayers I don't have the words for. Your peace that surpasses all understanding, let it guard my heart. In Jesus' name, Amen.

Write a prayer or any thoughts that come to mind:

Be still before the Lord and wait patiently for him.
Psalm 37:7 (ESV)

As a deer pants for flowing streams,
so pants my soul for you, O God.
My soul thirsts for God, for the living God.
When shall I come and appear before God?
—Psalm 42:1-2 (ESV)

THIRSTY

Read Psalm 42:1-2.

Hydrate, hydrate, hydrate! How many times have you heard that at a welcome center in a national park?

While the psalmist writes about a deer, if he lived nowadays, he might say, "As a hiker craves water when hiking in a desert, so do I crave the water only God can provide." That's my hiker's translation, but I think you get the point.

We've all heard stories of people who underestimated how much water they needed, and their bodies began to shut down. At the Grand Canyon, more people require emergency attention for dehydration than for falling. And if you've been to the Grand Canyon—with the amount of edge-standers and Instagram influencers risking it all for the perfect photo—that might surprise you.

Often, we can be like those hikers who think, *It's not gonna be that bad. We have enough water.* Yet we, too, can become spiritually dehydrated. The only thing that can truly satisfy our thirst is being with God.

The psalmist understood that just like water is essential for hiking—

especially in the desert—God is essential for our lives. We don't just need a quick sip once in a while; we need hydration.

In verse 3, we begin to clearly hear the desperation in the writer's voice: *My tears have been my food... Where is your God? These things I remember as I pour out my soul...*

Then he does what I call "preaching to ourselves." He begins to talk directly to his soul. *Hey soul, there is always hope in God.*

Often, in the 'easier' times, we forget hydration. We forget how much we need God in our lives. But when hard times come—when tears are our food—we're reminded of our desperate need for God to be our hope. Whatever season you are in today: Hydrate, hydrate, hydrate!

Prayer

Take a deep breath and let your heart settle
as you pray the following prayer.

Dear God, like the psalmist, I thirst for You. Remind my soul of its deep need for You. Lord, I meet You here today, in need of Your hope in my life. Satisfy my spiritual thirst. In Jesus' name, Amen.

Write a prayer or any thoughts that come to mind:

As a deer pants for flowing streams, so pants my soul for you, O God. My soul thirsts for God, for the living God. When shall I come and appear before God? Psalm 42:1-2 (ESV)

God is our refuge and strength, a very present help in trouble.
Therefore we will not fear though the earth gives way,
though the mountains be moved into the heart of the sea,
though its waters roar and foam,
though the mountains tremble at its swelling.
—Psalm 46:1-2 (ESV)

Day 13
TREMBLE

Read Psalm 46.

I'm not a worst-case-scenario kind of girl, but living in California, earthquakes are a real danger. I remember feeling the whole building shake one day in my third-floor apartment. Every worst-case event played out in my head. I remember thinking, *What if it all comes crashing down and I'm left with nothing?*

Maybe you take a peek at the news once in a while, or maybe you study it every day. Either way, we're never far from worst-case scenarios. The psalmist was looking around at nature—and he went there. He looked up at the mountains and thought, *What if my world is crumbling in every way? What if even the mountains disappear into the ocean?*

Yet we hear the tenderness of the psalmist as he goes there. But he doesn't just sit in the darkness of the mountains in the sea. He reminds his reader—and himself—that even if end-of-the-world catastrophes happen, there is still hope.

If I saw the tall towers of rock starting to fall near me, I would be terrified. Yet the psalmist offers us another way. He speaks of a sure foundation in God—a theology deeply rooted in a God who is present with us in the most harrowing circumstances, a God who shelters us when the rocks come crashing down, who ensures that our present suffering is not the end of our story.

I have a feeling you've experienced pain, grief, and hopelessness. As humans who live in a broken world, we have, are, or will experience it. So where do we run? Where do we go to find safety in those dark nights?

My prayer is that we find refuge, strength, and peace from the One who knows our past, present, and future—who simply says in the darkness moments, *Don't focus on the world crumbling around you. Look at Me. I've got you, daughter. I'm here and I'm never leaving.*

Prayer

Take a deep breath and let your heart settle
as you pray the following prayer.

God, when everything is crashing down around me, I need You to hold me. Refocus my eyes from the terror around me to Your arms of comfort and peace. Remind me of Your goodness in the darkest places. In Jesus' name, Amen.

Write a prayer or any thoughts that come to mind:

God is our refuge and strength, a very present help in trouble.
Therefore we will not fear though the earth gives way, though the
mountains be moved into the heart of the sea, though its waters
roar and foam, though the mountains tremble at its swelling.
Psalm 46:1-2 (ESV)

When I am afraid, I put my trust in you.
In God, whose word I praise, in God I trust;
I shall not be afraid. What can flesh do to me?
—Psalm 56:3-4 (ESV)

HAND TO HOLD

Read Psalm 56.

I'm afraid of heights. Nothing is more nerve-racking than walking close to the edge and looking down. I'm not proud to admit it, but sometimes I literally need someone to hold my hand. You got that, right? I'm a grown woman, and I need someone to hold my hand. I'll usually do it, but I will be deathly scared the whole time.

I first discovered this fear when I was a little girl. I walked confidently to the edge, and then I looked down. Everything in my body froze. I remember my mother calling me to come to her, but I couldn't move.

In that moment, I needed a hand, not someone to carry me, but a hand. I needed to know I was not alone.

Have you ever been in a spot like that? Not afraid of heights, but paralyzed by fear in your life—when you couldn't even take the next literal—or theoretical—step?

Maybe it was a relationship ending that shook your confidence in others. Maybe you've taken a good look at your life and realized that there are patterns of abandonment. So much so that, even though you thought you did, you no longer really trust others.

Don't worry, sister—I've been there. I've lain in my bed wondering if sleep would come, but instead grief continues to sweep over me while I sob violently from the complete destruction of the life I knew. I didn't even have the energy to get out of my bed.

In that moment, all I needed was to know I wasn't alone.

The psalmist recounts how he feels trampled, injured, and attacked, but even in that place, he proclaims: *When I am afraid, I put my trust in you.* In verse 8, he tells us that God keeps count of our tossing and puts our tears in a bottle. He sees you, and you are not crying in vain. You can trust that God is good, and that He does not waste your pain.

Prayer

Take a deep breath and let your heart settle
as you pray the following prayer.

God, life can feel overwhelming. Thank you for Your promise that my tears are being bottled and that You will not waste them. I need Your hand today to take my next step. When I'm afraid, I'm going to trust in You! In Jesus' name, Amen.

Write a prayer or any thoughts that come to mind:

When I am afraid, I put my trust in you. In God, whose word I praise, in God I trust; I shall not be afraid. What can flesh do to me?
Psalm 56:3-4 (ESV)

But I will sing of your strength;
I will sing aloud of your steadfast love in the morning.
For you have been to me a fortress
and a refuge in the day of my distress.
—PSALM 59:16 (ESV)

IN GOD I TRUST

Read Psalm 59 and 2 Chronicles 20:1-23.

David wrote this psalm while King Saul, the reigning king, had sent people to kill him. I don't think I would be writing a song if I were in his situation. However, in this psalm, we hear the heart of David—the confidence he had in God to deliver him. He had experienced God's deliverance before, and he knew God would do it again.

Worshiping God might not be the first thing that comes to mind when we're in a tough spot. Maybe you call a friend or go for a very long hike instead! But David sets an example for us: praise. Even when everything seems to be going wrong around you, praise.

Praising can be hard. It might feel easier to go into nature, ground yourself in it, and be with God that way. If that's your brand of connection, go for it! But I want to encourage you: praise God *before* the victory.

Have you heard of King Jehoshaphat? He was the King of Judah and followed God. He did many things to realign Judah with God, such as bringing back the priests in the temple and the public reading of God's word.

One day he was told that the Moabite and Ammonite armies were coming against him. In the middle of his threat, we're told that Jehoshaphat went to seek the face of God. God told him that victory would be his.

As Jehoshaphat prepared his army, he decided to lead a worship service. He praised God *before* the victory. As the singing and praise went up, God set an ambush against their enemies. The Army of Judah didn't even have to fight that day—because God fought for them.

Odds are, you're not facing a physical battle with enemies, but what battles are you anticipating? Maybe it's a lifelong struggle with mental illness, depression, or perhaps you know difficult news is coming. Whatever your current battle may be, I want to encourage you: praise before the victory.

Prayer

Take a deep breath and let your heart settle
as you pray the following prayer.

Dear God, I want to praise You. I might not see the victory today, but You have come through before and I am trusting You will come through again. Give me the courage to praise You in the uncertainty, knowing You are a good God who will bring victory. In Jesus' name, Amen.

Write a prayer or any thoughts that come to mind:

But I will sing of your strength; I will sing aloud of your steadfast love in the morning. For you have been to me a fortress and a refuge in the day of my distress. Psalm 59:16 (ESV)

Lead me to the rock that is higher than I,
for you have been my refuge,
a strong tower against the enemy.
—Psalm 61:2-3 (ESV)

Day 16

ROCK HIGHER THAN I

Read Psalm 61.

Do you ever feel small? Have you ever walked through Park Avenue in Arches National Park? If not, I highly recommend it. There's nothing like large rock formations towering above you to make you feel small. It's in moments like these that I think of Psalm 61:2: *Lead me to the rock higher than I.*

As humans, I think we all have the desire to be a part of something bigger than ourselves. More than that, I think we have an innate feeling that we need someone bigger than us.

St. Augustine of Hippo said: "Lord, you have made us for yourself, and our hearts are restless until they find rest in you."

We all have a hole in our hearts that only God can fill. We might try to stuff other things into that hole, but they will not satisfy us for long. We are made to need God. When we accept that we are small, and that God is bigger than us, only then can we truly live into our God-given identity.

I encourage you—the next time you feel small, embrace it. Take a moment to thank Him that you are small, and that He is big and protecting you.

Run to Him and let yourself be hidden in the refuge of a God who is good, who will shelter you as the storms of life pass around you.

The psalmist continues in this chapter by asking God to let him dwell in His tent forever. The tent of God was a symbol of the presence of God.

The psalmist is asking to sit with God forever. *I want to be near you, God.* He knew that the secret to life wasn't trying to do things on your own, but rather to rely on God.

So as you step into today, be reminded that everything is not on your shoulders. There is a rock higher than you, one who can hold steady in the storm, and you are invited to hide away with Him.

Prayer

Take a deep breath and let your heart settle
as you pray the following prayer.

God, the rock that is higher than I, today and every day, would You remind me that everything is not on my shoulders? I can find refuge in Your presence. God, I give You the worries of today. I accept Your invitation to be near to You and let You handle it for me. In Jesus' name, Amen.

Write a prayer or any thoughts that come to mind:

Lead me to the rock that is higher than I, for you have been my refuge, a strong tower against the enemy. Psalm 61:2-3 (ESV)

He alone is my rock and my salvation,
my fortress; I shall not be greatly shaken.
—PSALM 62:2 (ESV)

Day 17
NOT SHAKEN

Read Psalm 62.

Earthquakes are odd. You can't really do anything to prepare for them. They come out of nowhere and then disappear just as suddenly.

If you've never experienced an earthquake, odds are you have still felt that same loss of control in the middle of life's storms. In those moments, you become very aware that you are not in control—you're simply riding it out.

If you look up this passage in different translations, the words *I shall not be greatly shaken* often change to *I will not be shaken*.

But a little research into the original word tells us that it's actually the latter: *we will not be greatly shaken*.

Honestly, I think this phrase is more comforting—because we've all experienced shaking in our lives. Maturity isn't that we aren't shaken. It's about not being greatly shaken. Because our roots run deep. Our foundation is secure.

Liveable theology: what we believe about God and what we have experienced in our relationship with Him helps us when difficult times come. Do we choose to walk closely with a God who is good? Or do we believe God is malicious and delights in our pain? Do we truly believe God is good to us?

It's a question I've asked myself over and over again when earthquakes send tremors through my life. Can I simply sit in complete trust in God? Or will I try to control and minimize the pain that might come from the situation?

Will I surrender—so when the shaking happens, I'm not greatly shaken because I'm grounded in Him?

We have a choice. And trust me, the first few times the shaking happens, it's scary to simply hold on to God. But the more you do it, the less shaking in your life occurs. You begin to realize that you *can* trust in a good God to hold you steady.

Prayer

Take a deep breath and let your heart settle
as you pray the following prayer.

God my Rock, when my world is shaking, anchor me to You. When I don't understand what's happening, help me to believe in Your goodness. God, You are good and I want to trust You. Help my unbelief. In Jesus' name, Amen.

Write a prayer or any thoughts that come to mind:

He alone is my rock and my salvation, my fortress; I shall not be greatly shaken. Psalm 62:2 (ESV)

I think of you through the watches of the night.
Because you are my help.
—Psalm 63:6-7 (ESV)

DARK NIGHT

Read Psalm 63.

Dark Sky Parks are designated areas that restrict light pollution, helping to protect naturally dark night skies. In these parks, you can see the stars far more clearly than in the middle of a city.

Joshua Tree National Park is one of those places. At night, you can see stars you didn't even know existed—just as brightly as you can see city lights.

You have to go at the right time of the month to truly see the stars. If you don't, the moon's bright light will light up the sky like a huge flashlight. No headlamps are needed on those nights. You can simply walk easily among the trees. You can also see the coyotes *a lot* clearer on those nights.

The psalmist talks about meditating on God in the watches of the night. When I read this verse, I can't help but think about what the night sky looks like in these parks. The stars and the moon!

How else can it be explained except that a loving, all-powerful God created it all? There are definitely uses and reasons for all of it, but I'm not even close to being a scientist who could tell you why. Fellow nature lover, what I can tell you is this: I know that God made the world not just practically for us; He made it beautiful for us to enjoy, so that we could be reminded of His goodness in the stars and the skies. Even the night skies remind us to meditate on God!

You might not be in a dark park tonight, but here is your homework: take some time to look at the night sky tonight—if it's not raining! Just sit in the stillness and take in the goodness of God. As you look at the sky, ask God to bring to your mind the ways He has come through for you before. Think about the times He has been your help in times of need.

Prayer

Take a deep breath and let your heart settle
as you pray the following prayer.

Dear God, the Maker of the night sky, remind us in the quiet of the evening of Your goodness to us throughout the day. When I look at the stars, I can't help but feel small. I am reminded of how big You are and how great You are, and I want to remember You've got me. Even in the night, You walk with me. Remind me of Your promises. In Jesus' name, Amen.

Write a prayer or any thoughts that come to mind:

I think of you through the watches of the night. Because you are my help. Psalm 63:6-7 (ESV)

*We praise you, God,
we praise you, for your Name is near;
people tell of your wonderful deeds.*
—Psalm 75:1 (ESV)

Day 19

GIVE THANKS

Read Psalm 75.

Have you ever been so caught up in life that you forget to be grateful? Chances are, you have. Life can take so much energy just to get through the day. We can easily focus on all that's gone wrong instead of the many ways we saw God come through for us.

It can be easy on days we spend time hiking or being in nature—when our lives simply consist of what we are eating and how long the trail is. When life is simple, gratitude can be easy. But we can't always be in that peaceful place. We have busy lives that weigh us down, and seeing how God is working around us can be difficult.

The psalmist begins the psalm with thanksgiving to God. He is grateful for God Himself, for God's nearness, and His wondrous deeds.

Think back over the past week—about some wonderful deeds that God has done for you. You may start with the big ones: air, food, water, and life. God has been lavishing His blessings on you, often in ways you may not have even noticed.

One thing we definitely take for granted is God's nearness. Think back to the Old Testament, when the people of God had to make sacrifices just to come into His presence. They were not allowed to be near God because of their sin.

But today, because of Jesus' death, we are not only near God, but the Holy Spirit lives within us. We cannot go anywhere without the Holy Spirit being with us. Our God is not a far away deity who created us and moved on. He is *close* to us. He walks with us every day.

Yet often, we don't slow down to walk closely with Him. We're so busy trying to get things done that we don't take the time to walk with God and ask Him what *He's* up to. When we open our eyes, we can see all the ways God is providing for us.

Prayer

Take a deep breath and let your heart settle
as you pray the following prayer.

Dear God, open my eyes to see the ways You are working around me. Help me to slow down to walk closely with You. I praise You for Your wonderful deeds. Be close to me now as I desire to draw close to You. In Jesus' name, Amen.

Write a prayer or any thoughts that come to mind:

*We praise you, God, we praise you, for your Name is near;
people tell of your wonderful deeds.* Psalm 75:1 (ESV)

How lovely is your dwelling place, O Lord of hosts!
My soul longs, yes, faints for the courts of the Lord;
my heart and flesh sing for joy, to the living God.
—Psalm 84:1-2 (ESV)

Day 20
ONE EPIC DAY

Read Psalm 84.

Do you ever feel an itch or a deep craving to go somewhere? Maybe you've lived in many different places in your life. Have you ever felt the need to go to one place—or to return to one place?

Maybe you live in a big city like I do. Every so often, I need to go to the mountains. I need space, and I long to be near mountains.

The psalmist talks about his soul longing to be with God—and how it cannot be satisfied with anything else.

Yet we often try to satisfy that longing with things of the world— whether it's food, a good movie, or a book. The truth is, no matter how hard we try, our soul was made to be filled by God alone. So the next time you feel that itch—that sense that you were meant for something more—remember where true fulfillment comes from.

I love how he ends the chapter: *No good thing does he withhold from those who walk uprightly.* Do we really believe it? Deep down in our souls, do we believe that God does not withhold good things from us?

It wasn't until a few months ago that I finally wrapped my head around what it meant that God does not withhold good things. This also made me realize that I had been settling for less all my life. Instead of holding out for the best, I was trying so hard to control my life.

Maybe you have always believed that God has good things for you, and you've always held out for the best, no matter how uncomfortable. That's the hard part: the uncomfortable waiting. I wish I could tell you that the more you do it, the easier it gets. It does seem like God ups the stakes every time with me. He asks, "Do you trust Me now?"

Sister, I want to encourage you. God only wants to give you good things—maybe not the way we would see good things, but He desires to bless us.

Prayer

Take a deep breath and let your heart settle
as you pray the following prayer.

God of blessings, one thing I desire is to be with You. Increase my desire to be in Your presence. You only give good things. Right now I trust You even though I cannot see the future. You are in control. Give me grace and peace in the waiting. In Jesus' name, Amen.

Write a prayer or any thoughts that come to mind:

How lovely is your dwelling place, O Lord of hosts! My soul longs, yes, faints for the courts of the Lord; my heart and flesh sing for joy, to the living God. Psalm 85 :1-2 (ESV)

When I thought, "My foot slips," your steadfast love,
O Lord, held me up. When the cares of my heart are many,
your consolations cheer my soul.

—Psalm 94:18-19 (ESV)

PRAY WHEN OVERWHELMED

Read Psalm 94.

Have you ever walked near a huge drop and kept thinking that you were going to fall? Maybe you even imagined yourself falling down the huge drop.

As I mentioned before, I have a very intense fear of heights, so this verse feels personal. Yet, I love what the psalmist says: *O Lord, hold me up.* The image again of the Lord being so close and near to us that He would be holding us up.

The psalmist goes on: *When the cares of my heart are many, your consolations cheer my soul.* Have you ever felt that your cares were many?

In just one day, we can find enough cares to overwhelm us. If we just peek at the news, we can start feeling exhausted. Wars, human trafficking, poverty. Odds are, you could also just step outside your door and feel overwhelmed.

Let me bring it a little closer to home. What comes to mind when you wake up in the morning? What worries of the day come running into your mind the moment you wake up? If you're like me, your thoughts are just starting to come together. In those early moments, it's easy to feel vulnerable—like everything is in your hands to figure out and to carry alone.

I've started waking up to worship music in the morning because that's how I can remind myself that I need Jesus. The song I've been loving recently is entitled "Here Again." The lyrics say: *I'm not enough unless You come. Will You meet me here again?*

It's a simple prayer that's changed my life. It's an admittance that I need Jesus in the morning or else I can't do what He is calling me to.

Whether it's in the morning or another time, I want to encourage you to have a regular check-in time with God. He wants to hold your hand. He wants to cheer your soul and remind you that He is in control, and He is holding you up.

Prayer

Take a deep breath and let your heart settle
as you pray the following prayer.

Dear God, thank you for all the times You've upheld me and stopped me from falling. God, I need You. Comfort my soul when I think I can do it all myself. Remind me of my dependence on You, that it is not my weakness but my strength. In Jesus' name, Amen.

Write a prayer or any thoughts that come to mind:

When I thought, "My foot slips," your steadfast love, O Lord, held me up. When the cares of my heart are many, your consolations cheer my soul. Psalm 94:18-19 (ESV)

*As for man, his days are like grass;
he flourishes like a flower of the field;
for the wind passes over it, and it is gone,
and its place knows it no more.*
—P*salm* 103:15-16 (ESV)

Day 22

HERE TODAY,
GONE TOMORROW

Read Psalm 103:15-16.

Have you ever wanted something so badly that you held on to it too tightly?

The Bible tells us that our life here on earth is here today and gone tomorrow. It hit me one day—if we, as humans, are here today and gone tomorrow, how much more do our seasons come and go?

We all have a picture of what we want our lives to look like. Maybe it's a career, your dream job, or your dream relationship. Yet, in life, nothing is guaranteed. It's one of the harder truths in life to accept.

What could be an amazing relationship one day can turn on a dime. So what do we do with that? How do you deal not just with small disappointments, but with the large, soul-crushing moments that make you question what you're even good for?

Sister, I have a feeling you've had those kinds of soul-crushing defeats—where you feel like a withering flower that will never bloom again. Me too. I would love to offer you help in those moments, but

I have to be honest: those days still come and go more often than I'd like.

On those days, my only comfort is that God sees me. One of my favorite verses reminds me that God collects both our tears and our prayers. No pain in our lives is wasted. Yet in those moments, nothing makes sense. The spiral begins, and the next thing you know, everything feels upside down.

Even though we are like flowers, God cares so deeply for us. So when you feel like everything is out of control, remember: God walks with you. He has compassion for you. He sees you. Don't be afraid to reach out to God when you're spiraling. He will hold you close.

Prayer

Take a deep breath and let your heart settle
as you pray the following prayer.

God, I'm spiraling. I'm feeling lost. My soul is crushed. I need hope in this situation when I cannot see any way out. God, be near me as I grieve the past. I look forward to Your new calling. God, You are good, and I trust You. In Jesus' name, Amen.

Write a prayer or any thoughts that come to mind:

As for man, his days are like grass; he flourishes like a flower of the field; for the wind passes over it, and it is gone, and its place knows it no more. Psalm 103:15-16 (ESV)

Bless the Lord, O my soul! O Lord my God, you are very great!
You are clothed with splendor and majesty.
—Psalm 104:1 (ESV)

Day 23
PRAISE THE LORD

Read Psalm 104 and Exodus 14:14.

I love this chapter. I can't help but imagine the psalmist walking in nature as he wrote it—noticing creation all around him. He wasn't just observing everything around him; he was going on a gratitude walk. *Thank you, God, for this...for this, and even that.*

This psalm makes me want to take a gratitude walk too—to start thanking God for everything I see. *Thank you for this tall palm tree, for that rock, and for how You have placed them.*

There was a time in my life when everything seemed to be imploding. The future I thought was about to unfold was suddenly in jeopardy because I did the right thing and spoke up about an uncomfortable situation. I was powerless to do anything except wait.

Have you ever experienced something like that? When your life is falling apart, and it's painfully clear that you have no control?

The verse from Exodus came to mind, *The Lord will fight for you, and you have only to be silent.* So with all the strength I had, I took a walk—but not in a beautiful national park that shouted God's goodness. I just took a humble walk around my neighborhood with street lights, apartment complexes, and noisy main streets. It wasn't what I wanted at the time, but I didn't have the strength or money to go somewhere scenic like the beach.

My prayer before I took the walk was: *God, meet me in a tangible way.* So I walked. I looked around, and I thanked God—for the fence, the sidewalk, the rocks. I spent my walk looking for ways God was providing.

I highly encourage you to do the same. Sometimes we get caught up in the idea that we need huge experiences like national parks or beaches, and we forget that God can meet us in our neighborhoods, under street lights, oak trees, and on cement sidewalks. They all declare God's goodness.

Prayer

Take a deep breath and let your heart settle
as you pray the following prayer.

Dear God, help my heart to be grateful everyday. We can get carried away with the ordinary and not see all the ways You provide. Open our eyes to see You at work in and around us. In Jesus' name, Amen.

Write a prayer or any thoughts that come to mind:

*Bless the Lord, O my soul! O Lord my God, you are very great!
You are clothed with splendor and majesty.* Psalm 104:1 (ESV)

Oh give thanks to the Lord, for he is good,
for his steadfast love endures forever!
Let the redeemed of the Lord say so,
whom he has redeemed from trouble.

—PSALM 107:1-2 (ESV)

Day 24
STORYTELLING

Read Psalm 107.

Let the redeemed of the Lord tell their story. What's your story? Have you ever sat down and truly reflected on what the Lord has done for you? If you have, what feelings came up during that time?

Our story is a powerful thing. Too often, we don't take the time to sit and think back on the ways God has come through in our lives. In those moments, we can find comfort in knowing that our God always works things out for our good. It might not be the way we envisioned it, but as we look back, we can see how God was with us—even in the hard times.

How many times do we question whether *this* will be the time He doesn't come through? Maybe the situation feels so impossible to us, and we can't imagine how God can come through this time. Yet I am reminded that our God promises to be with us and to use all our uncertainty and pain for His good.

Sister, I don't know what season you're walking through today. Maybe you've finally seen the goodness of God in your life, and you're praising Him for providing in His abundant way. Or maybe you're about to walk into a season that scares you.

Maybe you're in the middle of the largest storm you have yet to see in your life, fully aware that you cannot calm it, that this storm is the darkest it has ever been in your life.

We might be tempted to wait until the victory to tell our story, but what if you tell your story *before* the ending is clear?

I never imagined how many other women had stories similar to my own. In telling my story, they found the courage to tell theirs—stories of redemption and God's goodness that gave *me* the strength to continue.

Maybe you've come out of the darkest night of your life, and now you're dancing in the light. Tell your story.

There are people all around us that need to be reminded of the hope we have in God, that He does, always, come through.

Tell your story... whatever season you're in!

Prayer

Take a deep breath and let your heart settle
as you pray the following prayer.

God, I thank you for my story, for the ways You always come through for me. Thank you for the ways You are coming through, and the ways You will come through in the future. I love You. In Jesus' name, Amen.

Write a prayer or any thoughts that come to mind:

Let the redeemed of the Lord say so, whom he has redeemed from trouble. Psalm 107:1-2 (ESV)

Your word is a lamp to my feet and a light to my path.
—Psalm 119:105 (ESV)

HEADLAMP

Read Psalm 119.

Have you ever done a night hike on a trail you've never been on? I will always remember my first—and only—middle-of-the-night hike in the winter in Alaska.

Because of flight delays, we headed out on our hike in the darkness, which is not a hard thing to do in Alaska, where winter sunlight is limited. I took comfort in knowing that at least the bears were hibernating.

As we made our way to the cabin, the hike was not easy. I had never been on a hike where the only thing guiding us was our headlamps. There was a whole lot of trust that went into that hike. We followed the path, and the headlamps helped us stay on it.

The psalmist tells us that God's word helps to illuminate our path. A question we've probably all asked ourselves is: *What is my purpose? What is my next step?*

You might be thinking, *Yeah, I get the concept—but the Bible doesn't tell us to buy this house, date this man, or take this job.* I agree. The Bible isn't that direct. But when we spend time in God's word, we do get directions. When it comes to big decisions, we are told that God will be with us.

With that assurance, we get to decide what God is calling us to. The Bible does tell us that we were made for a purpose. How we live that purpose is up to us, but we must live into what God created us to be. God also tells us who we should partner with in life.

God's word also comforts us in the different seasons of life. In seasons of waiting, we see many people in the Bible who are also waiting for a promise. God calling you to the unknown—stories like Abraham, Joshua, and Ruth—remind us of God's providence.

Feel like the world is against you? Welcome to the club. Jesus, David and others were hunted down by those who couldn't stand God's calling in their lives.

So my question for you is: How can you allow God's word to light your path today?

Prayer

Take a deep breath and let your heart settle
as you pray the following prayer.

God, I thank you for using Your word to light my path. When I am unsure about what You are calling me to, remind me of Your word. Let me not stray from what You have revealed in Your word. In Jesus' name, Amen.

Write a prayer or any thoughts that come to mind:

Your word is a lamp to my feet and a light to my path.
Psalm 119:105 (ESV)

The Lord will keep you from all evil;
he will keep your life.
The Lord will keep your going out and
your coming in from this time forth
and forevermore.
—Psalm 121:7-8 (ESV)

Day 26
COMING AND GOING

Read Psalm 121.

Have you ever heard of the Psalms of Ascent? They were the hymn book for the people of God as they journeyed to Jerusalem—songs they would sing on their way to meet with God at the temple.

It's with this in mind that we hear the words of the psalmist telling us that our God watches over us—a God who will keep us from all harm. Wait, did I misread that? The song says that God will keep us from evil or harm? Raise your hand super high if you've never had harm happen to you. Can we believe this psalm?

If you look at the root word here, it's usually translated as evil or wickedness. It's not telling us that God will keep us from disappointment or soul-crushing moments, but that He will keep us from evil. Evil cannot touch us. Why? Because God is with us when we go out and when we come in. It will not take our lives.

I wish it said, *God will keep every bad thing from our lives.* Don't you wish the same? That God would say, *That sad feeling is out. I am not allowing disappointment into My daughter's life.* But He doesn't.

The psalmist kicks off the chapter by looking to the mountains for help. Often, the mountains or hills were actually something to be feared. Whoever had the mountains or hills, the higher ground, was the person with more power. Yet he looks to the hills and thinks about God's deliverance in that moment.

I don't know where today's devotional finds you. I hope you live somewhere with hills or mountains. I pray that if you're walking through a dark season, that you look up at those mountains and find comfort. I pray that if you're walking through a season of lightness and happiness, that when you see those mountains, you rejoice in God's goodness. Wherever you are, I hope this psalm brings you closer to God—just as it did for those journeying to the Holy City.

Prayer

Take a deep breath and let your heart settle
as you pray the following prayer.

God, as I look to the mountains, I am reminded of Your protection. Though I walk through dark moments, You are with me. When I walk through happy moments, You are celebrating with me. Thank You for being my keeper! In Jesus' name, Amen.

Write a prayer or any thoughts that come to mind:

The Lord will keep you from all evil; he will keep your life.
The Lord will keep your going out and your coming in from
this time forth and forevermore. Psalm 121:7-8 (ESV)

I wait for the Lord, my soul waits,
and in his word I hope;
my soul waits for the Lord,
more than watchmen for the morning.
—Psalm 130:5-6 (ESV)

WAITING

Read Psalm 130.

Waiting...anyone else dislike waiting? There was a week in my life where I simply could not do anything. I had to just wait. I'd reported something, and now they had to investigate what had happened. I simply had to wait.

At first, I began to spiral. Are you catching a theme here? I decided that during the time I had to wait, I would use it to be with God—to go on walks and hash it out with Him.

Why do you think waiting gets on our nerves so much? Is it because we hate wasting time? I have a feeling it has to do with control. When we are waiting, we are not in control of what is happening.

Waiting reminds us that we cannot, no matter how hard we try, change what is happening. We often find ourselves waiting for a miracle—or for the clouds to break before us.

I still remember the time my sister and I got a permit for Cadillac Mountain in Acadia National Park. We got two, because everyone wants a sunrise permit—but just in case, we got a daytime one too. The night before, it was predicted to rain in the morning, so we decided to sleep in. But during the day, it was still misty around us. Still we told ourselves that once we're on top of the mountain, it would be clear.

Honey, the wind was blowing sideways, and you could barely see in front of you. I remember my sister asking if we wanted to wait a bit, in hopes that it would clear. We decided against it. But as we drove down the mountain, I couldn't help but think, *What if we were just a few minutes away from it clearing?*

I'm not saying it would have cleared, but I wonder if we often, in the waiting seasons, are just a few minutes away from the sky clearing. The waiting is painful...but what we're waiting for is worth it. If we spend our waiting with God, it is never wasted—and He promises He is always with us.

Prayer

Take a deep breath and let your heart settle
as you pray the following prayer.

God, when I cannot see hope in the situation I am in, remind me of Your goodness. In the waiting, would I linger in Your presence and find peace and comfort? Let me hope in Your word that I am not alone, and You are with me. God of comfort, be with me now. In Jesus' name, Amen.

Write a prayer or any thoughts that come to mind:

I wait for the Lord, my soul waits, and in his word I hope;
my soul waits for the Lord, more than watchmen for the morning.
Psalm 130:5-6 (ESV)

*I praise you, for I am fearfully and wonderfully made.
Wonderful are your works; my soul knows it very well.*
—Psalm 139:14 (ESV)

Day 28

MISTAKEN IDENTITY

Read Psalm 139.

Odds are, you've heard this chapter before—probably in women's ministry or at a girls' event. Maybe it had to do with self-image or our body types.

You are fearfully and wonderfully made. Yes, but I wish we really believed that. I grew up in a culture that praised a certain personality type while shaming another for being "too much." Without even knowing what was happening, I learned to make myself smaller.

Maybe you did this too. You quickly learned which parts of yourself were desirable—and you showed more of that side of you—while minimizing the other parts that were not well received. I think that as women we do this more often than we realize. We make ourselves smaller so that others don't feel intimidated or so that we can be accepted. But God never meant for us to live in a box—otherwise he would have issued one with us when we were born.

I've sat with so many women who have made themselves smaller or changed their interests just to fit in.

When I first moved to California, I believed that everyone would be as outdoorsy as I was, coming from Alaska. I was in for a rude awakening. Apparently, women especially did not fish or hike in the same way I did. A casual stroll on the beach was one thing, but climbing up boulders and mountains was another.

I'm not sure what part of you has felt unsafe, but I want to proclaim to you: Sister, God did not make a mistake!

You are wonderfully made—with all those things about you. God made you for a purpose, and you get to live into that purpose every day of your life.

The next time you're tempted to minimize yourself, I want you to hear these words: You are a daughter of the King. You are beautiful, worthy, made for a reason, and deeply loved by God. Don't let the other voices tell you otherwise. You are made for a purpose!

Prayer

Take a deep breath and let your heart settle
as you pray the following prayer.

Dear God, in the moments I don't feel like I'm enough, remind me who I am. I'm a daughter of the King, loved by You, and not a mistake was made when You created me. Give me the confidence to trust You when I feel less than. In Jesus' name, Amen.

Write a prayer or any thoughts that come to mind:

I praise you, for I am fearfully and wonderfully made. Wonderful are your works; my soul knows it very well. Psalm 139:14 (ESV)

Praise the Lord from the earth, you great sea creatures and all deeps, fire and hail, snow and mist, stormy wind fulfilling his word!

—Psalm 148:7-8 (ESV)

Day 29
GRATITUDE WALKS

Read Psalm 148.

Praise God for all of creation. Do you ever wonder what exactly earth looked like before God created all the different places?

One of my favorite places to visit near Los Angeles is Joshua Tree. On a recent trip, I was chatting with a friend who was visiting Joshua tree for the first time. She asked me, "How do you think God came up with the Joshua Tree?" I chuckled. A tree that isn't technically a tree, that only grows in high desert, and not just any high desert, but *this* high desert.

I let my imagination run a little and joked, "Do you think the Holy Spirit came to the Creation meeting with some sketches for Joshua Trees?" Of course this would not be good theology, but we laughed about how interesting it was that God created so many different kinds of trees. We should have taken that moment to thank God for the trees, but we didn't. Maybe you've wondered the same thing. How is it that God provides us with such a beautiful place to live?

The psalmist goes on to describe creation: the snow, the clouds, the fruit trees and cedars—all of it reflects God's goodness. He goes so far as to tell *creation* to praise God.

We would not be adventurous women if we didn't take the time to enjoy the outdoors. Sometimes we overcomplicate it. We don't have to be in a huge national park or state park to praise God. Even the spruce trees and the foamy waves call us to worship God.

Prayer

Take a deep breath and let your heart settle
as you pray the following prayer.

Heavenly Father, You have created such beauty all around me. Yet, I don't often take the time to thank You for Your creation. From the mountains to the waves, everything You have made is good. As I see Your creation, would You stir up gratitude in my heart for Your blessings in my life? Thank You for Your goodness. In Jesus' Name, Amen.

Write a prayer or any thoughts that come to mind:

Praise the Lord from the earth, you great sea creatures and all deeps, fire and hail, snow and mist, stormy wind fulfilling his word!
Psalm 148:7-8 (ESV)

Let everything that has breath praise the Lord!
Praise the Lord!

—Psalm 150:6 (ESV)

Day 30

PRAISE

Read Psalm 150.

Do you love worship music? Maybe you fall into the category of making a joyful noise, but I have a feeling that's not true about you.

I once invited a friend to my church who had never attended a Sunday morning church service like mine before. Jokingly, he said his throat was so dry from singing so many songs!

Maybe you grew up in church and have never noticed how many songs we sing, or maybe you're like my friend, surprised by how many songs we sing in church. Music is such an important way we connect with God. It reminds us of our smallness and God's greatness.

Yet there are probably days when you don't want to worship God. Maybe you're going through a dry season or a season of grief. We don't always *want* to worship God. I'm reminded of the story of Jesus as he entered Jerusalem, riding on a donkey.

The religious elite told Jesus to rebuke His disciples for joining in with the crowd saying, *"Blessed is the King who comes in the name of the Lord! Peace in heaven and glory in the highest!"* But Jesus tells them that if His disciples didn't cry out, the *rocks* would.

The psalmist says that everything that has breath should praise the Lord. So we *should* be praising God. I know there are days when we don't feel like praising, but if we don't praise, the rocks may cry out.

I think of the rock formations at Joshua tree, and imagine those rocks suddenly breaking out in song. I don't want to risk it—so we better be singing! Singing about the great things He has done for us.

Did you know that singing actually signals to your body that you're safe? Think about it—no one sings in a truly dangerous situation. The act of singing sends a message to your nervous system that all is well. So even on days when you don't feel safe, singing can remind your body of the deeper safety and peace that is found in God.

Prayer

Take a deep breath and let your heart settle
as you pray the following prayer.

Praise You, Lord, for all the ways You have come through in my life. Thank you for creation and all the beautiful things You created around me. You have been so good to me. Let me praise You in the storms and in the sunshine. In Jesus' name, Amen.

Write a prayer or any thoughts that come to mind:

Let everything that has breath praise the Lord! Praise the Lord!
Psalm 150:6 (ESV)

REFLECTION & GRATITUDE

As you close this 30-day journey, thank you for allowing these pages to walk beside you. It has been a joy to adventure with you—through reflections, prayers, and bold steps of faith. You are a woman of courage, created to explore life with both grit and grace. May you carry the spirit of adventure into every corner of your days, trusting that God is with you in every climb, every valley, and every breathtaking view. Here's to all that lies ahead—go boldly, live deeply, and never stop seeking the beauty in the wild and sacred path you're on.

Your sister in Christ,

Joy

ABOUT THE AUTHOR

Joy Scarpuzzi is the youngest of four and grew up in Illinois and Ohio. In her adult life, she has lived in Juneau, Alaska, Orange County, California, and now calls the Central Coast of California home. She is an ordained Pastor of Discipleship with a Master's in Theological Studies.

Joy seeks to allow God's love for her to shape every part of who she is and what she does. Whether she's leading a retreat, preaching a sermon, or backpacking with friends, she seeks to help people experience God in everyday moments and extraordinary landscapes.

She enjoys spending her leisure time hiking, watching sports—especially football—or exploring the outdoors with her friends. Whether she's on a new trail, playing pickleball, or planning her next adventure, Joy believes that faith is meant to be lived out loud—with courage, curiosity, and joy.

When she's not writing or leading, you can find her in deep conversations with friends, sipping matcha or chai while reading, and dreaming about the next national park to visit.

To connect with Joy, follow her on instagram: @joy_scarpuzzi

NATURE ILLUSTRATIONS
by Joy

1. Joshua Tree National Park
2. Arches National Park
3. Joshua Tree National Park
4. Canyonlands National Park
5. Morro Rock State Park
6. Arches National Park
7. Zion National Park
8. Bryce Canyon National Park
9. Bryce Canyon National Park
10. Zion National Park
11. Grand Canyon National Park
12. Cuyahoga National Park
13. Arches National Park
14. Acadia National Park
15. Capitol Reef National Park
16. Arches National Park
17. Lost Dutchman State Park
18. Joshua Tree National Park
19. Shannon Falls Provincial Park
20. Arches National Park
21. Bryce Canyon National Park
22. Bryce Canyon National Park
23. Canyonlands National Park
24. Lost Lake, Whistler
25. Capitol National Park
26. Bryce Canyon National Park
27. Mamquam Falls - Whistler
28. Joshua Tree National Park
29. Squamish, BC
30. Joshua Tree National Park